HiDDEN JEWELS OF HAPPiNESS

Skip Johnson

Powerful Essays for Finding and Savoring the Gifts on Your Journey

SKiP JOHNSON

Editing by Karolyn Herrera, DocEditing.com

Cover and interior design by Dino Marino, DinoMarino.com

Hidden Jewels of Happiness

Powerful Essays for Finding and Savoring the Gifts on Your Journey

Skip Johnson

CONTENTS

INTRODUCTION

Not too long ago I came across a photo that my daughter Betsy had snapped of me and my granddaughter, just as little three-year-old Adelyne reached up to grab my hand while we were walking down a quiet sidewalk on the outskirts of Atlanta. I didn't know she had taken it until she sent it to me the next day.

At first glance, it reminded me of the "Better enjoy the time spent with people you love" adage.

But as I looked more closely at the picture, I started thinking about the simplicity of the moment and how much was *right* during my short walk with Adelyne. Things I hadn't even noticed at the time the photo was taken.

In fact, I counted thirty-nine hidden jewels which had definitely been there and worthy of my appreciation, including

- the favorite pair of shoes I'd been wearing,
- the fact that I even had clothes to wear,
- the beauty of the little stone wall next to where we were walking,
- the fact that I could walk with her,
- the people we smiled at and spoke to who smiled back at us,
- the warm sunshine,
- the beautiful brick sidewalk,

- the blue sky,
- my daughter who took the picture,
- my friends who I had just seen,
- life experiences that had brought me to this point in my journey,
- the imminent lunch at my favorite restaurant,
- the fact that I am even here to experience these things...

My list went on and on and probably could have gone well over thirty-nine.

Which brings me to the idea I want to share with you in this book:

Missing how much good is actually going on around us is easy, even though sometimes very little seems to be going on. We can be so tightly bound by our current worries, stresses, fears, and beliefs of how things "should" be unfolding or what we "should" be doing, that the ever-present, ever-growing distractions cause us to neglect the wonders that are happening right before our very eyes. The constant "shouldness" can blind us to all the goodness.

We're looking ahead hoping for easier times or looking back with regret at how we could have done better. Meanwhile, life is quietly presenting opportunities for beauty, healing and growth all around us. And then in an irretrievable instant, we may potentially miss big gifts that were disguised as little things.

Let's start changing that.

This book also presents thirty-nine potential jewels. I've put together some of my most popular essays for this collection, and they are designed to help you savor your journey. To get the most out of wherever you are. To keep you focused on the inspiration all around. And to squeeze out every last drop of happiness even when it may feel like there is no happiness for miles around.

These essays about generosity, gentleness, strength, courage, faith, hope, love, gratitude, and many other traits will allow you to reveal and seize gifts which are often carefully hidden throughout your daily experiences.

To begin your trek, quickly count ten things around you that you're grateful for. Don't think about it too hard—just start counting. Now find ten more.

You've probably realized that your mood just shifted in the blink of an eye to a slightly higher level of happiness from a simple act of appreciation. Which is why you'll find gratitude reminders throughout the book, as with many of my books.

We'll practice noticing how much we have been entrusted with in each moment and looking for all the good in the present. Don't be surprised if you start to realize that these small routine things in your day are often exactly what you may have prayed about weeks, months, or years ago.

You'll likely find this type of proactive gratitude is a secret weapon for ongoing happiness and contains a spiritual element which can change our outlook on life. It can recalibrate our thinking, and diminish the frustration, resentment, and discouragement which somehow enters our lives each day and hinders us from happiness in the moment. Consider this habit an immediate cleaning of the slate.

In fact, as we fully pour ourselves into the present, we'll discover the magic of forgetting what's behind us, forgetting what's ahead of us, and simply savoring the sacredness of now. In that present moment, we experience our life and relationships in new, empowered, and enriched ways. Fully open. Fully engaged. Fully alive.

The process starts with that one kernel of genuine, focused appreciation, then the cascading effects of gratefulness take over. And we can do this any time we choose, with the same results.

So friends, my challenge to you is to commit to looking carefully at the ongoing scenarios that seem routine and I hope that you will begin to savor your experiences on a whole new level. Gently peel back the layers of *everydayness* to find that overlooked jewel right in front of you.

Who knows? Maybe you will even find all thirty-nine.

PART ONE

NEW BEGINNINGS, NEW DESTINATIONS

*"The beginning is the most important part
of the work."*

—Plato

WRITING A BOOK
OF OUR LIVES

What if I asked you to write a book about how you want your life to unfold?

Writing a book isn't that hard but the tricky part is writing an *impactful* book. The "book of your life" is already in you, awaiting your decision to write it.

Who do you truly want to become? What do you desperately want to do? Where do you wholeheartedly want to go? These are the challenging questions that lead to greatness and bring forth uniqueness in our stories.

To find real clarity and a beautiful end product, our thinking must be focused and deep. We must ask ourselves what we want—fully and without compromise. What resonates in our souls when these questions subside?

As we answer, remember this process must exclude what others have told us we should do or should be. Those suggestions very often become so deeply ingrained that they make it difficult to separate *our* needs from needs that *others* have projected onto us.

If we allow this projection to take hold in us, an element of fiction is gradually added into our story, which in turn dilutes our genuineness, which consequently diminishes the strength of our truth that we could otherwise boldly pass on to others.

Now is the time to recalibrate. It's time to make certain the words and vision are our own, so the story we are writing will be an autobiographical masterpiece when finished. Not just something we've thrown down on paper to say, "I did it."

Now is not the time to think small or be distracted. It's not the time to listen to the voice in our head saying, "What makes you think you can?" It's not the time to give in to our doubts, fears, hurts, discontent, or reasons why we can't do it.

Now is the time to find purpose and courage. Not only as a goal, but as the gateway to a new life. When we summon and fully articulate those goals, they become a statement. A decree. An ironclad proclamation of belief in ourselves that no one can take away.

When the vision is clear and ready to be acted on, the book will begin to write itself. The dream will become a beacon, constantly guiding us through the storms that will no doubt arrive to challenge us.

The opportunity is before us—let's write.

THE IMPORTANCE OF CHANGE

Change is difficult. In fact, if someone claims that change isn't hard, they are misspeaking or aren't emotionally invested in whatever they were changing from in the first place.

When we get to the point where the cost—financial or otherwise—of continuing in "the same old way" is more than the cost of change, it's probably time to change. Even if it takes a while to admit, we know what we must do—we MUST change.

Change is important for us and for everyone who depends on us and who are important to us.

The choice to change will come with potentially extended, agonizing pain. In fact, the bigger the change, the more pain that may follow. People may not understand, may not agree, and may not WANT the change. Which is why it takes a great deal of courage and why we so often avoid it.

But, my friend, we must. Taking the step toward changing something in our lives that we passionately believe is right—although frightening—keeps the world moving toward becoming a better place for us all.

And one day, sooner or later, we will realize the lonely, gut-wrenching decision to change actually changed each of us into exactly who we were always meant to be.

THE MAGIC OF NEW BEGINNINGS

Those of us who have started over or taken our lives in a new direction understand how difficult and gut-wrenching it often is. How mentally and physically exhausting and overwhelming it can be.

Many people choose to simply keep going down the same path because change and unfamiliar beginnings are stressful. They may tell themselves that if they just hold on, things will surely get better. So, they may patiently wait and wish that things were different, while also feeling like their lives are slowly passing them by.

Not too long ago, I talked to a young man in his twenties who had changed jobs in the auto repair industry. I asked how the move had gone for him.

"Well, it was really hard at first. I had to make some tough choices as I went into a business that I wasn't familiar with. My dad had advised me against it because of the lack of security, but I wanted the job so badly. The job I'd had previously was eating me alive with boredom. But it meant a paycheck, so I stayed in it way too long. When I finally got up the nerve to take a chance and follow my dream, it was one of the most challenging decisions I'd ever made."

I gently asked him if it had been a good move. He smiled and quickly replied, "Best choice I ever made. I feel free. I feel happy. I mean, even on the bad days I feel like I'm the luckiest guy in the world. And even though I'd been afraid and that first step was hard, once I took it I never looked back."

As we talked, I could tell how excited he was with his career change—except for one thing.

"My girlfriend is so proud of me, but she hasn't had the courage to make the same change. Right now, she's stuck on an assembly line like I was. She's doing the same thing she has done for years and all she has to look forward to is her week of vacation. It breaks my heart. She just can't let go because she's afraid she might fail if she tries to do what she really wants to do. I just want her to try."

This situation highlights the real, painful challenge of taking a step—in faith—out of our secure surroundings. With courage. With optimism.

But at some point, we must. Down deep in our souls we know we must. Otherwise, years from now we'll play the "if only" game. "If only I had tried. If only I had taken the risk. If only I had trusted that I could follow my dream."

Don't get me wrong—now might not be the time to change for some. But now is likely the time to *prepare* for the change. Or at least to take the first step to visualize, articulate, and document the dream that we have.

Time and life will come and go whether we courageously act on fulfilling our dreams or not. The clock is ticking. The sun rises and sets as it does each day, with or without our bold decisions.

Where do we want to go, and when do we want to see the magic begin? Today is the day to plan. Now is the time to start.

WHAT'S YOUR TRUE DESTINATION?

Henry Miller wrote in his memoir, "One's destination is never a place but rather a new way of looking at things."

"But my goal *is* my destination," you may say. Well, yes and no.

A goal or vision for where you want to go is key. When a goal is the result of a burning desire to achieve a result, powerful things begin to happen. But once you have that goal in mind and write it down, it's time to really pay attention to the rich, new experiences that are inserted into our journey towards that goal. As we resolutely move ahead, it's as if the universe is saying, "Good choice, now let's have some fun."

But we must be alert and astute on our adventure, so we clearly see the events that bring about the achievement of our goals. If our eyes and ears are open, we will start seeing those signs that are pointing us in the right direction. People, places, and things that we wouldn't have noticed before will now be our guides, gently nudging us on toward our destinations.

Honor each of them because they are mentors and each one has a very specific and necessary role to fill while helping us get where we want to go. Some are disguised as problems or extremely difficult decisions we must make, but we need all of them.

This new or renewed understanding that everything and everyone has a place in leading us to eventual success allows us to have gratitude for each piece of the puzzle.

Now is the time to decide where you truly want to go, and then trust that things will happen for you exactly as they should. You will eventually reach your destination while also realizing your true destination is who you have become as a result of the journey.

THE OVERLOOKED KEY TO REACHING OUR GOALS

Here's a little secret I learned from working many years in the health-club industry that most folks don't realize: You don't have to wait for the beginning of a new year to set and successfully achieve resolutions and goals.

Whether we're talking about fitness, finances, or a new attitude, we can start any time and get powerful results. But we need to do some specific things to achieve our goals, regardless of when we begin the process.

First, carefully think through your goals. Make sure you understand *why* you are setting those particular objectives and visualize how life will be different once you achieve them. Will reaching your desired goals give you what you *really* want?

If the answer is yes, the next step is to write your goals down. As you may already know, clearly documenting your intentions is incredibly powerful.

Now time for the hard but super powerful step. Slooowwww down, give up control and trust that your goals will be reached. Once we've formulated and documented our plans, one of the most challenging things in the process is to detach from the day-to-day need to control or force our dreams to fruition the way we think it should happen.

Quite often, people want to speed things up and make the results occur quickly because *surely* they know the best route to take to reach their goals…don't they?

Not necessarily.

It's not always our job to decide how we will reach our objective. More often, our job is to clearly set that objective and then allow the work to begin toward achieving it. No premature poking, stirring, or tweaking. Just wait. Because a much better, easier, or more effective way to get there than we initially imagined may appear. Once we crystallize our vision, if we are patient, everything will start working for us at precisely the right time.

This approach may seem lazy as if I'm suggesting we set our goals and do "nothing," but it's actually quite the opposite. This approach involves having the courage, strength, and discipline to believe our God-given abilities and wisdom will lead us to the achievement of our goals at the right time, and without stressing, forcing, and overthinking.

Definitely simple, but not easy.

It entails knowing that behind the scenes, things are happening to perfectly pull it together for us, sometimes without realizing it. The puzzle pieces are being moved into their proper places, but we must become patient and allow the process to work. The patience becomes a calmness and then becomes a relaxed manifestation of our faith.

Sure, we should periodically review our documented goals to keep them locked in our mind, but then let our creative minds and subconscious get to work for us. Each time we do, we will want to approach our review with gratitude and contentment— traits which overcome disbelief, fear, and anxiety.

Slow down, breathe deeply, and redirect away from the "what ifs." Trust your goals will be achieved and the path will become clear. If another path to a better goal exists, that will become clear as well.

Goals clearly defined? Check.

Goals written down? Check.

Goals achieved? Just wait.

PART TWO

GATHERING STRENGTH FOR THE JOURNEY

"We don't even know how strong we are until we are forced to bring that hidden strength forward."

—Isabel Allende

THE SPARK WITHIN US

For each of us, heart-wrenching times seem to suddenly appear on the horizon of our lives like terrifying, inescapable storms.

We will likely feel helpless, unprepared, and incapable of handling the force and impact these storms can have on us and our loved ones. It's as if a beautiful, warm fire that we have always drawn strength and comfort from is about to be washed away into a painful, horrible abyss.

But as the darkness envelops us and the driving rains seem ready to drown out every ember of peace and joy in our broken hearts, deep within us a small spark remains. It is so dwarfed by the chaos we feel that we don't really know the spark is there. But it is.

This spark is waiting to be gently fanned into a magnificent flame which can rise up in our life and bring forth a strength that is equal to anything we could ever face. It contains an unstoppable power that can generate courage, faith, and persistence that we might not have dreamed possible.

That spark waits patiently for us to believe in ourselves and in our ability to rise valiantly to the great challenge before us. The spark has been passed to us through the souls of our forefathers, who rose bravely to face their own frightening, lonely trials.

Today, if we are in the midst of the storm, we can take comfort in knowing that soon we will feel the spark of strength glowing deep within us. Take a deep breath through the pain and allow the spark to transform into a blaze that will take on every demon that crosses our path. We will tirelessly and courageously feel that fire change us forever.

HANGING ON TO OUR INNER PEACE

A short yet profound piece of advice from the Dalai Lama states, "Do not let the behavior of others destroy your inner peace." Seems simple to follow, but it's not.

Maybe what he was actually doing was providing a great self-growth opportunity. Energy draining people are out there and we can't change them, so let's be ready to change ourselves. And that's where the real power lies.

At first, we may not succeed in keeping their negativity from affecting our peace. But if we choose to become more aware and more prepared, each time they attempt to dump their potential stress on us, we can decide not to accept it. We'll get better at it a little bit at a time. Then better, and better. Until one day, instead of crushing or destroying our inner peace with their words or actions toward us, they will barely scratch the surface of our protective layers.

We'll begin to see that the beauty and uniqueness of who we truly are can't be taken away by someone else unless we allow them to. Our response to these disturbances becomes closer to, "hmmm, that's interesting—I see exactly what they are trying to do, and I won't buy into it," as opposed to, "my attitude and self-esteem are about to take a beating...again."

Curiosity replaces reactiveness. Gentleness replaces harshness. Peace and trust replace anger. Progress! We've now chosen to use our God-given abilities to rise above anything that's thrown at us.

Just like the ocean after a storm, the strong winds may have had a temporary, turbulent effect, but soon the calmness eventually returns. Those winds were simply necessary visitors who have now harmoniously disappeared into the past without a trace.

As we become aware of what's happening and resolve that our inner peace won't be available to those who try to take it, we'll notice something wonderful happen. Those once devastating winds that have come at us will transform into *welcome* visitors here to teach us where our soft spots are. They become harmless breezes that we now realize will blow in and out of our lives. As they go, they will leave us with the gift of increased strength and readiness for the next storm that will undoubtedly roll in.

Inner-peace stealers: bring it on—we're ready!

THE MYTH OF COMFORT

Two commonly expressed sentiments: "I really don't want much in life—I just want to be comfortable." "I don't need a lot of money—I just want to be comfortable."

Setting comfortable as our objective is like looking for the proverbial pot of gold. Once you go down that road, that darn rainbow goes on forever. And the more we seek comfort, the more we lose sight of the real pot of gold: a worthwhile path and savoring life along that path together with all of the challenges, pain, and imperfections.

You see, happiness disguises itself just as well as comfort promotes itself. We are often lured in, feeling certain that what comfort offers in its many shiny forms can bring us the contentment and fulfillment we really want in our lives. Comfort whispers in our ear, telling us that we need "just a little more" to really be happy, once and for all.

Meanwhile, happiness is modestly sitting in front of us in one of its many disguises: enjoying a heartfelt, nonjudgmental conversation with a friend; sharing a story with a mesmerized child; or doing a good deed at an inconvenient time without asking anything in return.

Yet despite all the richness in our midst, if we aren't paying attention, we often find ourselves focusing on all the things we *don't* have, and wanting things to be different, better and more comfortable. Then one day, we may look back and realize that the gold was in the middle of the rainbow we'd unconsciously been following—the exact circumstances we'd previously been in—all along.

Starting today, let's change that. Regardless of the many times we may have missed the happiness around us while we were searching somewhere else, let's commit to focusing on the happiness instead of seeking comfort, from this point forward.

My guess is we'll find more gold than we could have imagined waiting patiently to be found and claimed.

DOES GRATITUDE WORK? MAYBE, MAYBE NOT

We hear it all the time: "You should be more grateful." Yes, maybe that's true—but let's talk about it.

The powerful "secret sauce" of gratitude is its foundation in the most omnipotent force on earth: faith. If we choose to embrace the components of a grateful life, we are essentially tapping into the magic of faith. We are saying that we trust the path we are on no matter how challenging it appears to be.

Even if we're immersed in sadness or grief or pain, finding and incorporating an element of gratitude implies that we know everything is going to work out in our best interests and believe our current situation is a stepping-stone for even better things ahead. Despite the challenges, we have enough trust to embrace life and say, "Thank you."

Incorporating gratitude into our lives, similar to faith, is so simple if we choose to do it.

THE POWER OF "THANK YOU"

I've heard people say that when we learn to be consistently thankful and express that thankfulness, life can become a journey full of miracles.

Miracles? Really?

Meister Eckhart, the inspiring German theologian, likely believed the truth of this when he said, "If the only prayer you said in your whole life was 'thank you,' that would suffice."

At first this idea seems way too simplistic. How could those words have that much power?

Yet, when we say thank you, we express humility, deference, and respect. We admit the worthiness of appreciation. And when we appreciate, we acknowledge the good. When we acknowledge the good, we are expressing gratitude. When we express gratitude, we are seeing life through the lenses of optimism and faith. When we look through the lenses of optimism and faith, we begin seeing opportunities that we'd never noticed before.

Just like that, the world before us is now different and full of powerful, even *miraculous* transformations waiting to happen. And it began with the simple, authentic prayer: "Thank you."

GRATITUDE PITFALLS

What about during times when we choose gratitude, but don't get the results we expect? If gratitude isn't working for us, I believe it's due to the four following reasons:

First, sometimes our gratitude is conditional, which is not a good thing. We dabble in being grateful but are secretly comparing our lives to others' lives and hoping for a return on our gratitude "investment."

We talk about how grateful we are even though we really wish we had something else. Or we talk about how lucky we are to have certain things, people, and experiences in our lives, but still believe things would be better *if only* we could _____ (fill in the blank).

This contingent thinking dilutes the power of trusting that we are exactly where we should be right now. Conditional gratitude also puts the burden of control back on us. In reality, if we relax and are grateful where we are, we experience the bigger plan at work. If we're not grateful in our current circumstances, we'll never be fully grateful for whatever circumstance we find ourselves in later.

Second, we may say we are grateful while the rest of our life is out of sync with our words. We continue to use a vocabulary of shortage, instead of fulfillment and appreciation.

We lack a spirit of generosity because we don't trust we *will* have enough. We may not take time to invest in other people and their needs because we are too busy thinking about what we *really* need to be happy. We are tense and anxious, instead of taking our time, relaxing, smiling, and knowing that everything is working for us as it should. The antidote is simple—pure gratefulness, no strings attached.

Third, we aren't following through with our choice of gratitude. We give up too quickly.

Persistence is one of the most powerful traits and it applies to living gratefully as well. If we continue our efforts to live with appreciation, despite the times when gratitude doesn't seem to be working, we *will* start seeing powerful changes in our lives. But we must press on even when difficulties arise if we are to eventually see the fruits of our labor.

Fourth and finally, we don't believe gratitude will work for us; maybe for other people, but not us. Maybe some other time, but not now.

The wonderful thing about incorporating gratitude is that we don't even have to try very hard because gratitude is sitting there, waiting—and putting it to work in our lives takes little effort.

Gratitude is simply waiting to be chosen, wholeheartedly, and doesn't play favorites. When we do choose it, we will almost miraculously start noticing how much we have to be grateful for.

When we don't choose it, we'll continue to notice more and more reasons why gratitude doesn't work for us.

When we begin living in pure gratitude, we habitually look for how many things are going well, and for all the good in people around us. Trust and optimism become our dominant values. Our lives become filled with thoughts and things that bring us happiness and peace, and worries and anxiety fade quickly. People around us feel the difference in our attitude and the feeling is contagious.

Today is a perfect day to begin a new journey of belief, optimism, and gratitude. We don't need to wait until life is perfect or until conditions are fully acceptable. Waiting for the perfect life eliminates trust, faith, and gratitude and is a thinly veiled attempt at control. With that type of attitude, we will continue to wait longer for things to hopefully improve instead of perceiving all the good that is happening all around us.

In fact, if you are currently dealing with pain, heartache, or fear, this is the perfect time to practice being grateful and begin aligning yourself with a life of thanksgiving. My guess is you'll find that gratitude works for you like I have found it works for me—in a powerful, lasting way.

WHAT'S THE MESSAGE BEHIND OUR MESSAGE?

We all want to deliver positive, clear, and effective messages to people in our lives. But have you ever considered that maybe your words and actions don't always align with the principles you aim to articulate?

Consider the following communication approaches to ensure the right messages are heard by others.

In conversations, find something to agree on even when you have contrary opinions. No one likes to be told they are wrong, and if you can appreciate something in what the other person is saying—even if only to agree that they have the right to feel the way they do—you are much more likely to get your point across. Doing so would not be compromising your belief but allowing the other person the space to be valued and respected instead of immediately trying to convince them of your perspective.

Let's be sure we are living life as a fun, challenging game, instead of a great battle. When we see the world and our environment as an ongoing fight, then the typical battle-type scenarios appear. We start speaking and acting out of fear and focus on not losing. We lose creativity. We become more tense and frustrated. We refer to things we "must" do instead of seeing opportunities and possibilities. And we lose the fun.

If we communicate through an attitude of conflict and competition, our message will undoubtedly be interpreted through those filters and will likely be distorted.

Don't get me wrong—I am as competitive as anyone when it comes to desiring excellence. But when I choose to see my work and life as a challenging, high-level game instead of a dreary and tense fight, everything—including my communication—changes for the better.

Learn to relax more, laugh more, and play more each day, and don't wait until everything is perfect because it never will be. It sounds paradoxical, but even during times of stress and worry, the ability to see it as a necessary part of the "great game" will allow us to deal with our challenges in a way that is less stressful, more engaging, and more freeing.

Be the eternal optimist. Spread positivity and enthusiasm like crazy. As much as possible, be a cheerleader for others. Nothing can build camaraderie and raise the spirit like optimism and enthusiasm and knowing the person you are speaking with has your best interest at heart.

Oh, and don't complain. At all. It's a waste of time and doesn't do any good for anyone, including yourself. Complaining is a killer of enthusiasm, proactivity, and joy. If you would like to learn more about the power of not complaining, read *A Complaint Free World* by Will Bowen. I predict that it will permanently change you no matter how positive you think you already are.

Compliment specifically, genuinely, and often. Be on the lookout for anything and everything people are doing right, and you'll be amazed how much good you'll find. You may have to reprogram yourself to look for it.

Don't flatter folks insincerely and tell them how wonderful they are doing and how many things they are doing right if they really aren't. That type of mentality is not genuine or caring. In fact, it's an example of manipulation and people can smell it from a mile away.

Instead—carefully and authentically—find traits or actions you can recognize and honor in others. Remember, the greatest craving people have is to be appreciated, and folks are much more likely to listen to you if they feel valued.

As you develop these communication skills and display more confidence, compassion, and authenticity, you will ensure the message behind your message aligns with the outcome you desire. At the same time, this will allow you to connect with people on an astounding level.

PART THREE

SHARING THE JOY WE FIND ALONG THE WAY

"Choose to be optimistic, it feels better."

—Dalai Lama [Tenzin Gyatso]

WHAT I'VE LEARNED FROM RELAXED, HAPPY PEOPLE

Although everyone has their share of pain and difficulties, I've met quite a few folks over the years who have developed traits and habits that allow them to stay relaxed and often experience a higher level of happiness than many of us. I believe we can all adopt and benefit from these traits in our lives.

Relaxed, happy people are patient. These folks have learned not to rush themselves or other people. They have developed the attitude that everything is happening at just the right time, so there's no need to hurry. And since they are patient, they are freed up to slow down and savor the people, places and experiences in their lives, which just seems to increase their happiness.

They find the fun in life. They don't wait around for a problem-free life. Relaxed and happy people have an aura that declares "Hey, life is short and what I make of it so I think I'll make it fun." Everywhere they go, people seem to welcome them with open arms and open hearts. Why? Because through their relaxed and happy actions and outlooks, these people reflect to others how good life can be for all of us if we choose to see it that way.

They are generous. Really relaxed, happy people seem to be effortlessly generous. They understand that there is plenty to go around, so they are more than willing to share time, money, or resources to help other people. They've developed a mindset of giving, and they gladly look for and find opportunities to help all around them. Incidentally, the seeds of generosity they plant seem to come back later to nourish them.

They use low-stress, happiness-oriented language. They are optimistic and peaceful and choose to align their actions and words with that mindset. They thrive on sharing encouragement, and they talk positively about the small and large victories—not failures—of other people. Consequently, they seem to discover more and more goodness in their lives and the lives of others to enjoy.

They are content. Exceptionally happy, relaxed people know that an attitude of contentment and appreciation not only makes them and the people around them feel good, it connects them to an incredibly powerful world of love, kindness, courage, and trust. They don't keep score or compare what they have to what other people have. They're perfectly happy with their share, and since they know that comparing and contrasting doesn't help them or others, they avoid it.

Today is a great day to learn from these low-stress masters of happiness and incorporate their powerful traits into our own lives. So, smile, take a deep breath, and tap into these traits for a relaxed, happier you.

I LOVE ENCOURAGERS

My favorite people to be around are encouragers—people who cheer you on and who truly seem to want you to be happy and successful. In fact, if you screw up, they assume you were trying to do the right thing rather than the wrong thing. Maybe I appreciate them so much because that's the kind of person I consistently aspire to be.

Recently, I found out that a guy I have great respect for has been through an incredible amount of challenges and pain in his life. But you would never know it when you meet him because he smiles easily, laughs often, and spends his time looking for ways he can make other people, including me, happier and feel more valued.

And lo and behold—he is one of the happiest people you'd ever meet. You see, he has learned an incredible secret to a happier life: focus on diminishing the pain of others instead of on his own pain. And he does this regardless of the position or status in life of the person he is ministering to. Whether they appear to be more successful or wealthy, or someone who could never afford to repay the kindness, my friend encourages and supports their efforts and wins.

Feeling jealous or resentful of people who have more or who seem to have been dealt a better hand in life could be easy for my friend to do. Trying to make himself feel better about his own plight by downplaying the status and the success of others could also be easy to do in the situation. He could judge them as having more success simply because they'd been just plain lucky.

But that's not his style. He knows that outlook wouldn't help anyone and that this judgement about others would actually reflect poorly on him. On the contrary, his kindness and enthusiasm toward everyone he meets makes him welcomed wherever he goes. That positive energy fuels him to spread more and more goodwill and to become happier himself.

I have heard it said that only the truly strong can be kind and gentle. My friend has helped me realize that this is true. Only emotionally strong people have the ability to be compassionate and happy for others regardless of what they know about that person's journey.

Do you want to feel stronger and happier today? Make someone *else* genuinely feel stronger and happier today.

A CUP OF COFFEE AND SOME FLOWERS

S itting on my small table were two items: A simple cup of warm coffee, and a plain white vase holding a few colorful flowers. Not a lot there, right? Then again, maybe a lot *was* there.

As I sat in the little meat-and-three restaurant and waited on my lunch, I grasped how symbolic the flowers and coffee actually were. At that moment, I had found an oasis of serenity and simplicity in the middle of a highly stressful business day. Despite all the tense and demanding situations I'd already faced that morning, this therapeutic vignette of peacefulness was sitting right in front of me. It spoke to me, saying, "Stop and regroup, Skip. The game wasn't meant to be that hard. Remember what's important."

I suddenly realized that even though I couldn't control the people or swirling activity all around me that day, I really didn't need to anyway! I can't change the difficult people or situations I'm dealing with, but I can shift my thinking about them.

I can remember what's unshakably important to me: developing traits like compassion, patience, peacefulness, courage, gentleness, and gratitude. Ones that I can choose at any moment, in any situation. I don't have to get sucked in to the tension and drama that's presented to me. Strangely, a cup of coffee and a little bunch of flowers was the reminder I needed that day.

As I left the little diner, the young clerk at the register asked me the typical question, "Everything good today, sir?"

I answered with a grin, "I guess I would say that it was simply perfect."

THE JOY IN JUST BEING

Each new season I drive by a little old farm in the countryside outside of the town where I live near Atlanta. I seem to have a magnetic attraction to it. Rolling hills, a small, faded barn with a few horses roaming around, and a little home that is decades if not centuries old but still well taken care of by the owners.

Every season, the scene looks different. A different theme emerges, a different story waiting to be told. Each scene has a different color, light, and feel whether it's spring, summer, fall, or winter.

When I drove by on a crisp morning late last fall, the farm and its surroundings looked like a pristine example of simplicity. Almost all of the trees had lost their leaves, the farm was quiet, and the colors were soft and subdued. The barn, the animals, and the surroundings projected a feeling of pure acceptance of life as it is and of whatever it may bring—the antithesis of striving, fighting, and worry.

This view was a reminder that our lives are similar to the farm scenario. As with seasons, they are constantly changing, whether we want or accept that change or not.

We seem to be constantly trying to mentally and physically maneuver our lives to make things different, as we attempt to control our circumstances and outcomes and potential consequences. Almost as if we want to be omnipotent and try to stay one step ahead of anything life may bring us. The stress of figuring it all out seems to be never-ending.

Perhaps if we just stopped and decided to quit trying so hard to navigate our lives, we could find happiness and contentment right where we are. Just stopped trying to steer the river or even the boat. We could stop the merry-go-round and allow ourselves and others to make the choice to drop the burdens we carry and just *be*.

If and when we decided to do that, we might realize that the way to enjoy our lives more had been right there in front of us. Nothing else was needed except the choice to pause, look around us, and gratefully accept life as it is with no expectations or judgements.

As with the scene at the farm, we could realize that the simplicity of the moment is where the real peace resides—always waiting patiently for us to find and accept it. Look for your own scene of simplicity and contentment today. It's likely closer than you think.

ARE WE SUCKING THE FUN OUT OF LIFE?

We all want to be happy. But at times we get so stressed, overwhelmed, and discouraged, that we begin focusing on everything going wrong and take our focus off all that's going right. This can cause our journey to happiness to derail in a big way.

Unfortunately, we begin focusing on avoidance and fear and worry about more potential problems. It's a vicious cycle and we should be aware of three symptoms that we might experience prior to wandering off the happiness trail:

WE FIND OURSELVES WAITING TO BE HAPPY

We may have gradually developed the belief that if we wait long enough, we will get out of our rut and life will start being fun and adventurous. Once we start a career, get married, have children or grandchildren, or retire—then we can REALLY start living! But waiting for someone or something else to bring us good times is like waiting for our car to give us better driving skills. Waiting is pointless. The solution is to recalibrate and realize that we are the only ones who can make our lives better—and then do it.

WE'VE BEGUN FIGHTING AGAINST LIFE

Sounds crazy, right? But when things aren't going the way we want, we often try to force things to get better. We start feeling like a victim and resist and fight the current situation to try to change it. Our words, actions, and thoughts become more tense and desperate. We seem to be in constant conflict. We argue about things that really don't matter and we correct other people just so we can be right. We complain to anyone who will listen. We find ourselves wandering through a maze of frustration and resentment when we could simply put the world down and trust that our lives will unfold in a beautiful way without the need to force or fight anything at all.

WE ARE TAKING, INSTEAD OF GIVING

When we begin to feel a decrease in happiness, it's often accompanied by the need to be recognized more. Instinctively we start exhibiting behaviors that we think will lead to more appreciation, but often at the expense of what brings us the most happiness: generosity. When generosity decreases, our self-gratification desire increases—and the trend just continues.

Each day when I get up, I ask myself three questions: What can I give today? What can I be grateful for today? Who can I genuinely thank today? This habit helps me to start off the day with a spirit of giving because I know that generosity is the antithesis of the messages received throughout the day to "get" and "have" to affirm our self-worth and self-confidence. Generosity not only strengthens the receiver but is a powerful manifestation of trust.

This spirit of selflessness and trust leads to unlocking our God-given abilities to live our lives with peace, joy, and personal power.

Becoming aware of these early signs should help you notice any happiness derailment, so you can practice some of these ideas and get the train back on the track and continue on your journey. Safe travels!

GENTLY SHAKING THE WORLD

Mahatma Gandhi once offered, "In a gentle way, you can shake the world."

"Shaking the world" may be the end result of a compassionate, tireless caretaker's actions. It could be the result of living with dignity and kindness through a debilitating illness. It could involve reaching out to include the lonely among us. It could also involve using our unique business or trade skills to help improve someone else's life. When we use our gifts to impact people through generosity, gratitude, and compassion, we can "shake the world."

Putting our pain and discontent aside and living in a way that brings peace, love, and strength to others without expecting anything in return begins a flow of selfless kindness and empowerment. That trickle becomes a steady stream and eventually becomes a powerful wave that shares the fruits of our labor in ways that would astound us if we knew how far-reaching they'd been.

As we immerse ourselves into pouring our gifts into the lives of others, we may one day realize that the world that was gently and positively shaken was as much ours as theirs. How will you begin to gently shake the world today?

PART FOUR

POWERFUL CHOICES FOR STAYING ON COURSE

---

*"We cannot become what we need to be
by remaining what we are."*

–Max DePree

STAYING OUT OF THE PEOPLE-FIXING BUSINESS

One of the chapters in *Grateful for Everything* is about "Retiring from the People-Fixing Business." This concept involves attempting to control or "fix" people in ways that are often so subtle that we don't even realize we are doing it. These actions affect our happiness as well as the person we're intent on "improving."

My advice is to stop this habit sooner rather than later! The problem with people-fixing is multi-pronged.

First, obviously, other people don't like it. People-fixing or feeling the need to tell folks how it ought to be done is disempowering and eventually leads to resentment, anger, and unhappy relationships.

Second, we typically don't have the full context of the situation we are trying to give advice on. Even if we do, chances are we haven't truly and empathetically thought through their situation to the length that they already have.

Third, taking on another person's burdens and giving advice without being asked doesn't allow the individual to grow or find creative solutions on their own. It's spoon-feeding at best.

Finally, even if our motivation is just wanting to help, we inadvertently take away the most powerful desires all individuals have—to be valued and understood—when we step in and tell others what to do.

In fact, when we give unsolicited advice, instead of fulfilling the true needs of the other person, we have actually made an unconscious attempt to satisfy our own needs.

Avoid these four phrases to prevent continuing the "let me tell you what to do" habit:

1. "You should." For example, "You really should do what I say, or you'll likely make a HUGE mistake." *Should* is one of those words that so easily enters our vocabulary that we begin to use it constantly without noticing. *Should* implies that our proposed idea is correct, and that any other idea is definitely not the right thing to do.

2. "If I were you, I would…" The assumption is that you're the expert and certainly know the other person's situation well enough to make a better judgment than they could.

3. "All you have to do is…" Here the implication is that the answer is so simple, that if they won't just listen to what you're saying and do what you tell them, they are a dummy.

4. "See, I told you…" Yikes! The control-oriented aspect of this phrase is only outweighed by its borderline passive-aggressive undertone. It's like telling them that they should have realized they needed your advice to succeed and that next time they'll listen if they want any chance of surviving the situation.

Okay, now that we know what NOT to do, here's what we DO want to do to exit or never enter the people-fixing business:

Realize that we are not and cannot be "in their shoes" completely. Listen. Ask questions. Show compassion and empathy. Give strength and support. The most powerful thing you can do for another person is to simply believe in them and encourage them through their challenges and life in general. They will remember, and you will become empowered and self-confident as you learn how to genuinely help by not overly helping.

Now you've got plenty of tools to keep you from engaging in the wrong kind of fixing. So, use them to improve both your communication, and ultimately, your relationships.

OUR PAIN CAN BECOME OUR POWER

Those of us who have experienced loss or devastating events in our lives, understand that when the pain hits, we feel as if we have suddenly been thrust into a harsh and lonely land with no escape. In some ways, that may be true. But if we can learn to react bravely and hopefully to our deep hurt, lessons will emerge to transform the pain into permanent, powerful qualities.

Not only can these characteristics be healing for us, they can provide encouragement, empowerment, and healing to other people around us. As we choose to learn and grow through our difficulties, three key qualities will become part of our core being.

PATIENCE

It's easy to be patient when life is flowing in the direction we want it to. But when a tragedy or crisis occurs—all bets are off. We want to run from the pain and our feelings to return to normal as quickly as possible.

Yet, it's precisely during these times of crisis that the lasting growth and transformation in our souls will occur when we choose to be forbearing despite an almost impossible choice. For the great statesman, Ben Franklin, to have said, "He that can have patience can have what he will," the magical results patience can bring must have been clear to him. But they don't come quickly or easily.

EMPATHY

Our personal pain allows us to feel sympathy for other people and their challenges and to genuinely understand their sadness. Consequently, our ability to be compassionate and make a difference in their lives dramatically increases. When we observe others dealing with their own challenges, we now comprehend their situation and are far better equipped to provide help and strength.

PEACEFULNESS

Although it sounds contradictory, the development of a peaceful spirit can often occur during times of stress and hardship. By making the difficult choice to let go when we want to try and control it all, we will find ourselves in a state of peace and acceptance which builds a foundation of courage, strength, and love in our lives.

If we can open our hearts to the potential that lies within our crisis by learning to embrace the pain calmly and persistently, the lessons will gradually take root in a way that wouldn't happen by any other route.

We can then become part of that elite group who have stayed the course, kept the faith, and shared in the powerful, transformative benefits.

TAKE BACK YOUR PERSONAL POWER

I understand—life can be tough. In fact, sometimes our problems seem to suck the personal power right out of us. Work. Finances. Health. Relationships—at some point, each presents challenges to us. The good news is, we can recalibrate and take our personal power right back.

First, let's become students of life again, instead of teachers. Many of us feel that we need to have all the answers even when we weren't asked for a solution! We get into the habit of thinking that we need to know what to do and say in all situations, and even start trying to show others what we feel *they* ought to do. This habit is a real power drainer.

Instead, let's start learning to listen again, to be present and understanding, not all-knowing. You will be amazed at how it feels when you are confident enough to promote yourself to a constant learner, instead of a perpetual leader. Allowing others to solve their own problems is also empowering, by simply providing our encouragement and belief in them.

Second, remember that "easy does it." With all the potentially stressful people and situations we deal with, finding ourselves tense and anxious much of the time is not surprising. Beginning to let go and breathe slowly and gently can help us relax and gain more power, rather than through clenching our muscles and trying to force things to go the way we think they must. Another better way probably exists, but we must let go to find out.

Third, using the wrong words will *definitely* harm us. The more disempowered and inadequate we feel, the more we begin to unconsciously reflect those feelings through our word choices. When we use pessimistic words, we feel even worse and the downward spiral continues.

Switching to powerful, confident, optimistic words breaks the cycle, and will almost immediately begin reversing the negative feelings. Soon, our positive words and feelings of empowerment are back in sync.

Fourth, we must take care of ourselves. Flight attendants always advise us, "In case of an emergency, when the oxygen masks drop down, put the mask on yourself first." Essentially, each time we allow someone to take away our personal power IS an emergency and a time of potential happiness we won't get back.

Take small steps toward prioritizing self-care through things like daily inspirational reading, regular exercise, proper nutrition and positive interaction with people you love. By having the courage and commitment to strengthen yourself first, you will regain the power to use your skills and abilities to better help others.

Today, let's commit or recommit to developing these habits. With a little practice, we'll likely find they will unlock doors that will swing wide open to welcome us to empowerment, encouragement, and self-confidence.

THE PERFECTION OF IMPERFECTION

Beauty: a sunset, a blue ocean, a snowcapped mountain. "Beauty is in the eye of the beholder" we've been told. But what if we began to dig deeper to find beauty that we may have missed at first glance?

We would learn not to ignore a lot of the things that we take for granted every day. We'd learn how to appreciate beauty almost anywhere we go, in everything we see or do. For example, that dilapidated farmhouse that you pass on the way home each day—instead of passing it off as the eyesore it appears to be, you might wonder about all the years a family had spent there. The children that were raised. The birthdays and holidays celebrated. The pets that were loved.

Or the piece of furniture in your house that you've walked by for years. You might consider how durable it is and stop to notice the craftsmanship that originally attracted you to it—instead of breezing past the "outdated old thing" you'd planned on getting rid of.

Instead of complaining about the leaves that are falling on our fresh lawn, we could appreciate the colors and shapes and crispness of each one.

The Japanese have a term for this—wabi sabi. Finding perfection within things typically perceived as imperfection. The slight crack which adds character and history to the beautiful porcelain cup holding your morning coffee. The wrinkles, gray hair, and less than perfect physiques that cause us angst. Maybe they're also cause for a gentle celebration that God has allowed us to live long enough to have those characteristics we fight so hard against.

Wabi sabi is finding beauty in seemingly imperfect places. If we look beyond appearance, beauty seems to be everywhere we gaze. Once we realize that, our happiness, compassion, and contentment will begin increasing in response to our new outlook.

Take a fresh look for yourself. I'm sure you'll agree with me that there's plenty of perfection all around you.

MAKING OUR OWN HAPPINESS

I hear it often: "Yes, I know I make my own happiness, BUT you don't understand what I'm dealing with."

"Yes, I know I make my own happiness, but you don't know my past."

"Yeah, I know I make my own happiness, but I just _____ (fill in the blank)."

We all consciously or unconsciously put off our happiness for reasons that we've convinced ourselves should keep us stuck in discontentment. So much is going on, so many bad people are in our lives, we have so much stress and pain, and there are so many decisions weighing on us, that it seems impossible to find happiness, much less create our own happiness.

Struggling and feeling pain and disappointment is perfectly fine and even healthy, BUT here's a simple, powerful antidote to help us move beyond feelings of helplessness and discouragement:

Change the word "but" to "and."

"Yes, I have a million things to do AND I will get them done one at a time at the perfect moment."

"Yes, some people in my life seem determined to make me miserable AND I am stronger than anything they can throw at me. I welcome the challenge!"

"Yes, I face challenges in my life AND each of them is a lesson to make me a stronger, wiser, more compassionate person."

When we throw away the reasons why we can't be happy, suddenly we realize that we have found untapped strength to meet any difficulty or pain we may face.

Today, let's choose to be in charge. We are bigger and stronger and more courageous than any challenging situation we are facing or will face. "I make my own happiness AND I'm starting right now."

CHOOSE TO THRIVE, NOT SURVIVE

Each day, we are required to make a huge decision which we often don't realize we are making. A decision that provides the foundation for all the other smaller choices we will have to make each day, week, and month for the rest of our lives.

This important decision is to choose whether we want to thrive or simply survive. Whatever we choose is going to dictate how we see the potential in our relationships, business, and lives in general. It will set the levels of our belief, courage, determination, gratitude, and virtually all traits that lead us to success.

I vote we should choose to thrive because once we do, we'll begin tapping into the expansive possibilities that result from believing we are able to take control of our lives. We'll be declaring that the power to achieve what we want is truly in our hands. We'll start seeing the practical reality of life's most pressing problems happening *for* us, not to us.

Once we make the choice to thrive, we will view everything and everyone that appears in our life as an ally for greater wisdom, compassion, and strength, as opposed to just another thing to deal with.

The world as we know it will change. At that point, any fire that we are thrust into becomes fuel for living life at a level that we didn't know was available or attainable. Simply surviving would be lowering the bar for our God-given gifts and potential.

Yes, we will still face challenges, but it really won't matter because now each has a perfect place on our path to the greatness we have chosen. Courage and compassion, not anger and resentment, become our tools of choice.

As we are presented with difficult situations and people, we will magically see we have exactly what we need to face them and flourish. Imagine the freedom!

Today we'll accept everything that comes to us as part of the process, fueling our powerful, courageous, and infinitely capable lives.

Today and from now on, it's time to thrive.

PART FIVE

VALUABLE TOOLS AND GUIDANCE

"Change the way you look at things and the things you look at change."

—Wayne W. Dyer

THREE POWERFUL TOOLS FOR OUR HAPPINESS JOURNEY

Let's begin a never-ending adventure to an inspired, enriched, happy life.

Whether we say, "The joy is in the journey" or "Treat every day as your last" or "Carpe diem," the desire is to get every drop of fun and joy out of living that we possibly can.

Going on this trek doesn't mean we have to be extroverted or overly-enthusiastic, but we do have to be willing to start looking for the great experiences that are hiding, just waiting for us to find them.

Even in the most mundane, routine places, the potential for savoring experiences can be found. And we want to find it as often as possible. Learning to see our lives as "the great game" instead of simply "fighting the daily lousy battle" is necessary.

To head out on this great adventure we have to be properly prepared. We must have the right tools and equipment, or it'll be a disaster. If we aren't prepared, we'll start wandering aimlessly, get discouraged quickly, and end up with nothing more than a short-lived personal pep rally.

And that's definitely not the path we want to take.

Let me share with you three of my most valued tools, my best lessons learned on how to avoid the unfulfilling and unnecessary detours as often as possible, and to maximize the adventure of life.

They may not be perfect, but I assure you they are tried and true. In my experience, they are critically important and have made a powerful difference in my life. When I use them properly and consistently, my journey is amazingly rewarding.

Before we get started, it's important to know that WE WILL BE FACED WITH OBSTACLES on this trip. In fact, this journey to a new way of looking at life is not for the faint of heart. People may try to distract you, take from you, hurt your feelings, or worse.

But you're ready—you're laser-focused on your mission to live a life of happiness and adventure. And your life doesn't need to be moving along perfectly when you start or as you continue this trek. In fact, the messier and more challenging our lives are, the more helpful and strengthening this view of the world will become.

NON-COMPARISON MINDSET

First, start locking in the mindset that you will not compare *your* journey with anyone else's. You don't know what someone else's life is like, but I assure you, it's not easy for them. You don't know the battles they face behind the scenes, and you certainly wouldn't want to base your presumptions on the pictures of the ideal life we see on social media.

In fact, that concern is irrelevant when it comes to how successful your expedition will be. Your journey is yours and yours alone—owning that gives you great freedom. Focus on your own path and realize that making comparisons doesn't help us or others. Everything you need to succeed is inside you. You don't need the approval of someone else and you don't need to measure up to the perceived or apparent success of anyone else.

RESILIENCE

Secondly, we need resilience. We need to become mentally tough because this journey is difficult. The mountains can be incredibly steep. An unexpected terror may be around the next corner. But when we continually remind ourselves that we are tougher than anything that can be thrown at us, we begin to believe it. A little bit at a time, we become aware of our innate toughness.

Yes, we will get fatigued. People will try to trip us up on the trail. We will feel discouraged. But we are stronger than any of this—and we must constantly remind ourselves of that.

In fact, each of us has more toughness than we may even realize. Those of us who have been deep in the bowels of despair from trauma or life events and survived know that we each have an innate superpower that is waiting to be tapped when necessary. I have been there too, my friends, and I know this strength exists for each of us.

On your journey, when events seem impossible to escape or navigate, remember you are prepared.

OPTIMISM

Finally, our new adventure will require us to become diehard optimists. Life's happenings are neutral, but it's worth repeating to ourselves that *we* get to choose how we see each event.

Yes, there are exceptions, but the real pain and suffering more often than not comes about when we take the neutrality of situations and attach layer upon layer of our interpretations, fearful stories, and doubt to them. Even when events are extremely painful, we can often lessen the length and severity of our pain by learning to change the story we tell ourselves *about* that event.

In our new adventurous way of looking at the world, our stories can change to passionate, grateful ones of life that is preciously short and worth living. We can create and nurture those stories every day and become happier people, ready to impact the world in a new way.

But we must be patient, trusting, and open to looking at circumstances differently than we have in the past.

Shakespeare's *Hamlet* wisely stated that "there is nothing either good or bad, but thinking makes it so." Sounds simple enough to think that way but some people will not welcome your new optimistic way of thinking. They'll see you leaving their comfortable, pessimistic party and won't like it. But you've got bigger plans, so you can stand up to them and politely share words of appreciation for the invite, but make it clear you're heading a different direction, and can't make their party after all!

Speaking of words, this optimistic way of life is clearly reflected in our language. If it's true that our words create our world, then our words are also fuel for our journey.

Use words of gratitude, selflessness, and empowerment. Words that will supercharge your trip to the top of the mountain. Say "thank you" often, "I appreciate you," and "I'm proud of you," and warm words that produce joy and sustain our energy for the journey plus give energy to others.

Our words to friends, family, and everyone in general are a reflection of who we are and a preview of who we will become. They can inspire us and others, or they can do the opposite. Use them wisely.

We can't afford to slip into conversations full of gossip, cynicism, or criticism—they won't work with our new lifestyle. Doing so would be like putting oil in our proverbial gas tanks.

These tools—Skip's Tips for the Trip, you might say—can help us overcome challenges and scale new heights on our journey to a happier, more fulfilled, more exciting life: a non-comparison mindset, a commitment to resilience, and diehard optimism.

While reaching the destination is certainly a great goal, keep in mind something Jaime Tardy said: "The journey is the fun part."

Let's go have some fun!

THE ONE UNSTOPPABLE TRAIT WE CAN ALL DEVELOP

One characteristic can change our world in the same way that it has already changed the world of countless brave souls in all occupations and walks of life.

Persistence.

Enacting this trait can overcome fear, anger, insecurity, anxiety, frustration, sadness, disbelief, and negativity. In fact, I believe persistence is one of the most important traits one can develop for a successful and happy life.

Persistence can push through our doubts when we feel discouraged, lonely, and misunderstood. It can tear down obstacles confronting sales people and entrepreneurs who believe passionately in what they are doing but haven't yet expressed that successfully to other people. It can often play a critical role in helping athletes achieve their childhood dreams.

Persistence can strengthen a student who is struggling with their grades or battling the stress of earning a degree they have always wanted to achieve. It can bring courage and hope to caretakers for ill family members and give hope to those going through financial, health, or relationship struggles.

No matter our occupation or abilities or position in life, persistence can enhance us in ways that make us nearly unstoppable.

Because when we truly believe that nothing can defeat us, then nothing *can* defeat us.

Reaching our goals may take more time than expected. We may have to start over with a project that has taken us years to bring to fruition. We may need to find another route to complete our journey, but persistence will push us to where we ultimately need to be.

Thomas Edison observed that "many of life's failures are people who did not realize how close they were to success when they gave up." Indeed, persistence often not only separates the good from the great, but the happy from the sad. Those who are willing to try one more time tend to find the fulfillment, joy, and success that they aspire to because they overcome their fears and keep gently pushing on the doors of their dreams until they open.

Whatever obstacle we face today, let's decide that we will be doggedly persistent. In fact, in every situation where we feel the fatigue of potential loss, failure, or disappointment starting to weigh us down, let's make a pact with ourselves that we will press on through each and every challenge. The achievement of our goal is waiting for us, likely only inches away.

THE ATTRACTION
OF GENTLENESS

The trait of gentleness is incredibly attractive. Maybe it's attractive because it comes from the deepest, most tender part of a person's heart. A gentle person courageously reaches out and expresses their appreciation and their value for themselves when they show they value others. Their motives and actions are genuine as they feel no need to try to control, manipulate or gain perceived power by trying to make others feel less powerful.

In these "better get as much for yourself as possible" times, this gentle personality seems rare because it requires great strength and self-assurance. A person of gentle character exudes, "I know that in some way you're struggling, and so am I, so let's get through this whole thing together. It's all going to be okay." Deep down, we all want this reassurance.

But when we become gentle, we may initially feel vulnerable, which can seem frightening. What if we get taken advantage of? What if they don't reciprocate?

Those questions never occur to the truly gentle person because gentleness has become so inextricably woven into their lives. Displaying gentleness is no longer an action to them, it's a non-negotiable, unalterable lifestyle. The response a gentle person receives is almost irrelevant to them.

If kindness is reciprocated, bravo—more fuel for the gentle person and validation for the recipient. If not, the sandals are dusted off and the gentle person moves on. The power of true gentleness is that it draws its strength from the power source of love, faith, and compassion. So, if their gentleness lapses, they simply "plug back into the source" with no loss of power.

Today, through the kindness of listening, and through our words, prayers, mannerisms, actions, and interactions, let's enter the realm of gentleness. The world is waiting.

AVOIDING THE THREE THIEVES OF HAPPINESS

Our stress and pressure seems to escalate every day. In fact, *something* is almost always trying to steal away our happiness. Limiting and disempowering beliefs we have about people, places, or experiences continually cause us to be stressed, frustrated, or angry. These types of beliefs are absolute happiness thieves.

Well, never fear. Today we are going to beat back three of those stinking happiness robbers and learn how to keep them away for good. The ability to keep them from tarnishing our happiness and contentment is right inside of us!

Here's how to keep three of the sneaky rascals at bay:

HAPPINESS THIEF #1:
THE BELIEF THAT LIFE IS ALWAYS JUST SO HARD

You may be thinking, "Skip, you don't know what I have to deal with every day." Correct, I don't. What I do know is that each of us deals with challenges that we are *so sure* nobody else understands. We each fight those battles in different ways.

But here's a little secret that can bring us all some comfort: Life is often as difficult as we choose to make it. The French philosopher,

Émile Coué, reminded us to approach each task as if it were easy, and that belief would make it so.

You see, most often *our relationships to our tasks cause us stress*, not the tasks themselves. But we are told that we MUST try harder and we MUST fight through our problems and we MUST realize that life is just plain tough and it's always going to be that way. And we buy into that.

Things seem harder, we become tense and overwhelmed, and our stomach knots up thinking about how much we have to do and how hard it's going to be and soon—it's too much!!

Life then becomes a self-fulfilling prophecy of problems, pain and frustration. Every day, everywhere we go we feel the need to pick up a weapon and fight. We start looking for more things to go wrong and for more problems to appear, and they do. Which creates more stress and worry and feelings of overload.

Try this instead:

Realize that everything that happens in our life is preparing us for the rest of our life. Decide that the problem we are facing is simply the next task that has been placed in front of us to deal with. Nothing more, nothing less. As we deal with a situation, choose to see it as more of a great, high-level game, a personal challenge, and part of our life's adventure.

Strangely enough, our stress levels will likely start dropping, we won't apply the labels "difficult" or "hard" nearly as often, and we'll start to experience more of that relaxation all around us!

Start using easy words. Terms like "can't," "won't," "need to," "have to," "never," and "hate" lead to feelings of angst, disempowerment, and victimization. On the other hand, each time we use optimistic words like "yes," "opportunity," "believe," or "appreciate," we build a cushion of softness and relaxation into our lives.

In reality, life will continue to place challenges in front of us—often exactly the lessons we need to learn—and we will get through them, one way or another. We can withstand them kicking, screaming, and complaining, or we can choose to walk through them to their completion patiently and optimistically, and choose to learn their lessons.

HAPPINESS THIEF #2: THE BELIEF THAT WE MUST COMPARE OUR LIVES TO THE LIVES OF OTHERS

This happiness thief is super sneaky. Comparisons come in so many forms, and of course social media has supercharged this thief. Through comparison, we buy into the belief that "If only I had something else, then I would be happy."

The problem is, the imagined ideal is typically not reality and even if it became reality, it would have its own inherent problems. I'm a huge believer in setting goals. However, the unrealistic type of comparison ignores everything going right in our present lives. It makes us think that our *real* happiness is off in the distance and we'd better go get it—fast!

But remember, life doesn't have to be perfect for us to be happy. Never has, never will.

The real antidote to comparison? Again—gratitude. Nothing is more relaxing than living a life of gratitude. It is a manifestation of the belief that we already have plenty—and if you look around, you'll likely agree with me. Sure, having more or different things or experiences is always nice, but when we realize the gift that is inherent in our current reality, we begin looking through lenses of appreciation and happiness everywhere we go.

Life seems just fine—or better than fine—the way it is right now. If you have read some of my other books, you know how powerful I believe gratitude is. It's an incredibly effective tool for resisting this happiness thief.

HAPPINESS THIEF #3:
THE BELIEF THAT WE MUST MAKE OTHERS HAPPY

This thief is really, really annoying.

We are typically taught to be kind to people, which is always commendable. But what if we are kind to people, yet they don't respond like we want them to? What if they don't like us? If they don't respond to our kind gestures, it's certainly our fault, isn't it? Isn't it our responsibility to change that outcome? Oh no, we'd better try harder. We'd better be nicer. We'd better do more.

The more we try, the more tense we become and the more we wonder if *we're* the problem. We end up in a pointless, no-win cycle. We start sacrificing our own happiness by trying to make sure that the other person is happy—hoping that making them happy will surely make us happier.

What a mess. Someone else's happiness is certainly not our responsibility. Instead, maybe we should ask ourselves why we feel the need to gain their stamp of approval in the first place.

These people pleasing tendencies are more aptly called people *dis*pleasing tendencies. We are so worried about the people we are *displeasing* that we totally forget about all the people we *have* pleased. We raise the bar for approval from others to such a high level, we can never measure up, yet we feel we should still try. So, we try, and try, and try—even at the expense of our own happiness.

If we look deep enough, we'll understand that people pleasing is really a form of people fixing. When we try to fix people, we are trying to manipulate or guilt them into behaving like us or behaving the way we think they should. But fixing people always has consequences—either in the short run or in the long run.

Whether we are people pleasing or people fixing, we are attempting to influence their feelings or allegiance to bring them in line with our own goals or behaviors. Yet at the same time, we are making our happiness contingent on their approval or their response. Once we start that, the happiness thief has taken us down another dangerous path.

The perceived control we think we have over other people is usually based on our own insecurity and is essentially an illusion. In fact, maybe we are all fine exactly the way we are. No need for approval, no need to improve anyone else—just pure acceptance of ourselves, others, and the way life is.

Now that'll definitely keep those pesky happiness robbers away!

Let's continue discarding these limiting beliefs, and simply choose to be happy. As we do, we'll soon realize a rewarding sense of freedom, empowerment, and fulfillment that no happiness thief can take away.

THE HIGH COST OF IMPATIENCE

The shore of a remote little spot on Jekyll Island, Georgia called Driftwood Beach is a beautiful place to take photos. The beach is covered with petrified trees which create a unique environment that attracts people like me from all over the country.

If you stand on Driftwood's edge and look to the north, you'll see something else that's equally as fascinating. About a mile away, just off of the coast of St. Simons Island (where I was born), the underside of a gigantic freighter that capsized several months ago is visible. Fortunately, no one was hurt when it turned over, but its cargo of more than four thousand brand new cars was lost into the sea when that happened.

As I stood on the beach one day, looking out towards the ship, the enormous irony and contrast between the ship and the beach became very apparent to me. The cargo instability that led to the freighter disaster was supposedly caused by human error—a lack of patience and not following the correct course of action.

Driftwood Beach, on the other hand, is a model of patience. Nothing has moved or really changed for thousands of years. Rude tourists, stormy weather, and times of need have not phased the beautiful beach as it remains peacefully present and allows life to come and go all around it. Paradise lost. Paradise found. None of that matters to the beautiful driftwood found there. Whatever happens, happens.

Years from now when the big ship is gone and life has gone back to normal for people in the area, Driftwood Beach will continue to carry on patiently, waiting for the next chapter.

Patience or impatience. Today, let's choose wisely and watch paradise slowly but surely emerge in our lives.

CRAZY RULES FOR A HAPPIER LIFE

When I write and speak on happiness, I'm typically straightforward. But today I'm attempting to sneak in my message through some surprising rules. After reading through them, I think you will understand how these principles can quickly make a positive difference in your life.

BE JUDGMENTAL

Yes, judge everyone you meet. Judge them as competent, caring, kind people who are doing the best they can. Judge them as people who are fighting battles you know nothing about. Judge them as people who will be friendly if you are friendly to them. If they reciprocate your gesture, you win. If they don't reciprocate, you've taken the high road of virtue, and you still win.

BE SELF-CENTERED

So often when things aren't going well in our lives, we start looking for people or things to place blame on. Instead, start looking within yourself and use these situations to increase your strength and take your courage to a new level. As you reach those new levels, you will see how events and people in your life start reflecting those changes proportionally. You'll start becoming the change you want to have around.

TALK ABOUT PEOPLE BEHIND THEIR BACKS

Talk about them in a complimentary way. Few people have the courage and security to spend time sharing words of encouragement and affirmation about others if they know those words may never be heard by the one they are speaking highly of. But praising others when they are not around is uplifting to you, the person you are speaking with, and anyone else nearby. Practicing this just a little bit each day will greatly improve the way you feel and the perception others have of you. Besides, the listener is reminded that when they aren't around, you're probably speaking well of them too!

Now that you know the rules, it's time to act. Start applying these concepts throughout your day and notice how you feel more empowered, content, and crazy happy!

JOIN ME IN GIVING UP

Want to join me in increasing our personal power to a new level?

If so, then starting right now—let's give up.

Yes, let's give up the ideas and old beliefs that no longer serve our new vision of success and happiness, and replace them with a way of life that is rich and incredibly fulfilling, forever.

Let's give up being hostage to the haunting phantoms of fear and regret and replace them with an empowering mindset of courage and faith.

Let's give up the bitterness of holding on to our losses and embrace our new path toward a life of growth, opportunity and making a difference in the lives of others.

Let's give up the heavy weight of anger about things and people that we can't control, and replace it with the light, easy, and healing choices of forgiveness, peace, and trust in the outcome.

Let's give up actions and words of defeat and hopelessness—even the subtle ones—and choose words and deeds of strength and optimism instead.

Let's give up tension, anxiety and bracing for the next potential catastrophe, and instead begin to breathe slowly and deeply in the expectation of life's next gift.

Let's give up our preconceived notions about the way life should be and look instead at the countless blessings that we've been given and watch how gratitude can change us and those around us.

Let's give up thinking, talking, and acting fearful and small, and instead focus, speak and live in terms of greatness—however we choose to define it.

Let's give up believing that life is a dreary daily battle, and instead choose to live, laugh, and see each day as a great adventure.

Let's make the choice right now to give up all of these unhealthy ideas and actions and discover the world as we know it will never, ever be the same.

PART SIX

FACING AND EMBRACING OBSTACLES ON THE PATH

---

*"In the middle of difficulty
lies opportunity."*

—John Archibald Wheeler

DON'T THINK ABOUT YOUR LEGACY, DO THIS INSTEAD

I recently heard someone say they wanted to leave a great legacy. Something about that comment struck me, and I thought about it a lot for the rest of the afternoon and have often thought about it since then. Here's why I think focusing on legacy isn't such a great idea.

First, focusing on leaving a legacy is a lot like focusing on winning a trophy. Concentrating on earning a trophy equates to simply chasing success, an abstract goal. This takes our eyes off the goal in front of us, causing us to be so concerned with how we'll be honored and perceived, that we miss the real joy of being fully engaged in our tasks, living in the present moment, and trusting the outcome.

We erroneously view how we want to be remembered as the end game and forget the most enriching end game is the fulfillment that comes from acting on the opportunities and needs all around us that are begging for our full attention.

Second, we have a lot less control over our legacy than we may realize, which is actually okay. Even if we have control over our actions and our decisions and how we engage with life, the ultimate outcome may be different than we envision.

In fact, the past is full of people who had a great desire for posthumous fame or legendary status. Yet often history chose a very different perspective of them, people misunderstood their aims, or life's superseding plans got in the way of their goals. When legacy is the focus, we can't always control the outcome.

What is the alternative? Making the choice to live as we want to live, beginning right now. Embracing the present and winning by putting our hearts into living out our core values. Making a list of how we want to greet each dawn and go through each day, and then passionately doing just that. Living with appreciation, trust, courage, enthusiasm, and love. Deciding that the only thing we have in life is life at this moment and understanding that no one else is in control of that—not our friends or our families or our co-workers or anyone else.

The sooner we really believe this, the sooner we are on our way to living a life we were destined to live and one that will create a powerful ripple effect in this world. Let's agree to let our legacy be the by-product of how we have chosen to embrace life, instead of the goal of our life.

Regardless of decisions we've made or things we wish we had done differently up to this point, we can start living now—no matter our age or our abilities—by embracing and embodying all that is important to us.

We may feel an aliveness and a freedom that we've never known. We will be making the choice to be the captain of our souls and take full responsibility for our joy.

And who knows, we may just end up leaving a pretty nice legacy, too.

TRANSFORMING OUR DIFFICULTIES INTO MIRACLES

Turning our problems into miracles sounds like an impossible goal, doesn't it? It's tough enough to just hang in there and figure out how to cope with our challenges. To make something miraculous out of them—how in the world could we do that?

Although our problems may cause us to feel pain, if we choose to bravely dive into those problems and begin considering ways that something beneficial could come out of them, the benefits will appear. Maybe sooner, maybe later, but it will happen. Maybe we can only find a glimmer of something that may somehow work to our benefit. But start with that glimmer.

I know it's hard but dig, then dig deeper.

Looking for benefits doesn't mean we should or would be able to avoid the pain—it will still be there. But bravely stepping outside our difficulty—even briefly—prepares the "soil" of our life for growing our miracles. Now is the time to plant—not after years have gone by when we'll look at what came out of our crisis in hindsight.

After planting, then add the ingredient of gratitude for anything we're able to find within that painful challenge that can now potentially serve us well in the future. Not appreciation for the difficulty necessarily, but for what can come from it. This distinction is important because those who tend to shy away from speaking of gratitude during stormy weather can never fully appreciate the sunshine when it finally appears.

Expressing gratitude can help us turn the tables on our adversity and use the situation to our advantage to become stronger, wiser, more compassionate people. Even if our gratitude only comes in slivers at first, we can use those slivers as tools to build us a full-fledged fortress of thankfulness for the lessons. The more things we find to be grateful for, the more we can embrace our challenge as a powerful teacher to be welcomed, rather than avoided.

Responding in this way takes the power away from the problem and puts it where it belongs—with us. In spite of the pain, we courageously proclaim that our attitude and decision to grow through the pain cannot be taken away unless we allow that to happen.

Slowly but surely, we become alchemists—change agents. We effectively "miraculously" transform the difficulty life has given us into something that fuels us with a God-given power that will serve us and help us serve others in need. We become miracle workers—bravely manifesting courage and strength and love out of what seemed nothing but a dire, hopeless situation.

Today, instead of fighting our challenges, let's embrace them as our opportunities to begin our shifts as supremely courageous workers—miracle workers.

GETTING BACK TO HAPPINESS

Over the last year I have sought out and talked with some incredibly happy people. Through many insightful conversations, they shared with me how they regained happiness when they weren't feeling quite so upbeat.

Three of those approaches are quite simple—if we just remember to use them.

FIRST, BREATHE

When we become super-stressed, we actually hold our breaths, often without realizing it. This oxygen deprivation affects our mental clarity and physical relaxation and reduces our endorphin level, fundamentally diminishing our happiness.

Breathe slowly, gently, and deeply and you will feel the change of state almost immediately.

NEXT, SLOW DOWN

As we start feeling more tense, we tend to push ourselves to do things with more haste and less focus, which leads to more mistakes, stress and anxiety. One of the happiest people I've interviewed said, "The only thing I try to do in a hurry is return myself to a slower mode when I realize I'm hurrying!"

NOW, REMEMBER TO SMILE

In his powerful little book, *Smile: The Astonishing Powers of a Simple Act*, Ron Gutman talks about an incident as a young traveler in Central Africa. Gutman shared how he was on a bus in rural Zambia with no cell phone, no ability to speak the native language, and no idea how to find a safe place to stay as night approached in a very dangerous part of the country.

He recalled how important his smile had been to connect with people in other cultures. "I smiled at everyone around me. I smiled indiscriminately, I smiled widely, I smiled continuously. Whether people looked at me or not, I smiled at them." By using the simple and universal power of a smile, Ron was able to connect with a very kind older African woman who took him home to her family where they provided him safety.

Our smiles tend to disappear when we feel stressed, and then we tend to feel worse, and more stressed, causing us to smile even less. The cycle continues until we break it. And when we break it, we feel great!

If you're looking for a happiness pick-me-up, breathe, slow down, and smile. It works.

FINDING THE GIFT IN WHERE WE ARE

As we go about our daily lives, something interesting and significant occurs that we are often unaware of.

We are either using language, taking actions, and living out behaviors that reinforce our happiness and contentment or that reinforce our discontentment. Whether we realize it or not, the latter behaviors come with a high price.

As we are exercising at the gym, we may think about how badly we wished we looked different. As we are driving, we might daydream about how we wish our partners or friends understood us better. While we are at social gatherings, we may often notice how much happier all the other people seem to be. And as we glance at the magazines alongside the grocery checkout lane, we surely notice how much more fulfilled and stress-free the people on the covers appear to be.

Some days we might lose weight, get a raise, or receive great compliments—all rewarding, wonderful events. But, what about the portions of our life during which things like this don't happen? We can become caught in the trap of wasting precious time and energy hoping that *tomorrow* our lives will certainly be more satisfying and fun and rich. Meanwhile, the clock keeps ticking away.

Here's the incredibly powerful alternative: We can rise up and choose to find the gift in where we are, right now. Even in the most challenging environments, we can find opportunities that will be life-enhancing. Chances to inspire others. Ways to impact people with our skills and talents. Gifts, reminders, and gentle lessons embedded everywhere, yet hidden in ways that require us to look through new lenses to find them.

When we do, we leave the arena of waiting, worrying, and dreading, and enter the arena of thankful, unshakable, and empowered living.

The recipe is simple. Start with new, sincere words of encouragement for those who could use them. Then, add a healthy dose of consistent gratitude where we previously may have had the tendency to complain or be cynical. Mix in smiles and sprinkle on liberal doses of gentle laughter, and presto! We're prepared to start appreciating life as it is.

Today, even as we inevitably daydream of different or better things in our future, let's enjoy a whole new level of contentment, fulfillment, and growth *where we are now* by simply making the choice to find the gift.

TODAY IS THE DAY WE'VE BEEN WAITING FOR

Today is the day we've been waiting for if we choose to see it that way.

Today is the day we can begin living the way that we've aspired to live—joyous, courageous, empowered, and embracing the moments as they come to us.

Today is the day we'll realize that we are in charge of our own happiness and there's no one else to blame for not having enough. Today we will see that we aren't held hostage to other people's need to manipulate or change us in any way. We see clearly now that those desires are simply projections of their own insecurities and struggles and have nothing to do with us, so we'll easily and persistently rise above them.

Today is the day we will see life differently. Instead of seeing potential problems everywhere, we will see beyond them to the beauty, fun and opportunities that are all around us.

Today we will enthusiastically start taking care of ourselves so that we will live more fulfilled and become more capable of helping others do the same thing. Doing this is not selfish—it's wise and effective.

Today is the day that we will begin living with gratitude. Not comparing "up" by wishing we had what others have or comparing "down" by gloating about how much more we have than others, but simply being appreciative for what and who we have in our lives. Living with gratitude lays the foundation for noticing more and more of the positive.

Today is the day we begin living peacefully in our words, actions, and lives in general. We'll quit fighting, arguing and resisting the way things are. Instead, we'll embrace the challenges in our current situation to help us learn lessons for reaching our goals.

Today we will find contentment even within our discontentment, knowing that this too shall pass, and we'll be more prepared and compassionate people because of it.

Yes, today is the day we've been waiting for—a wonderful beginning to a whole new life. Let's begin right here, right now.

PART SEVEN

UNEXPECTED DETOURS

"We are all faced with a series of great
opportunities brilliantly disguised
as impossible situations."

—Charles R. Swindoll

The five following essays were written in the spring of 2020, during the coronavirus pandemic: one of the most challenging times in recent American history.

WHAT WILL WE LEARN?

What if we woke up tomorrow and the novel coronavirus was totally gone? What if it had somehow disappeared and life as we'd known it returned? Each of us should ask ourselves, "How did we use this pandemic to become stronger?"

Life is likely not going to return to normal any time soon. In fact, we may be headed for a new normal—like one we have never experienced before. If that's the case, will the personal growth choices we make during the pandemic make us better prepared for the new normal? Or will we simply get through it while complaining and worrying, spreading bad news, and waiting for it to be over, like many other people?

You may realize that we have been preparing for this all along. Not for the coronavirus specifically, but for life. Preparing ourselves mentally, emotionally, and spiritually to handle whatever crisis life throws at us. Preparing ourselves to be stronger than anything that comes our way. Now we have the chance to prove it. We have the chance to look life straight in the eye and say, "I'm ready."

Being prepared doesn't mean there won't be pain or prolonged challenges that make us weary and frustrated and discouraged. It simply means we are taking control of our attitude and know we will get through this time as stronger, wiser, and more compassionate people because of our choices to do so.

The virus will eventually leave. But it will be replaced by something else. A divorce, a health problem, the death of someone close to us, and so forth. If we don't use this crisis as an opportunity to grow and become better and more powerful, then we will become the victims the press makes us out to be, as well as unprepared for life's next curveball.

Here are a few ideas for how to use this time to recalibrate, then make significant progress toward a happier and more empowered life.

BEGIN LIVING GENEROUSLY

During a time like this, it may sound odd to start thinking more of other people when we are worried about issues we're personally facing. But that's exactly why we should do it. Because if we can be generous now, we can be generous any time.

Don't feel that your money can be stretched any more than it is? No problem—tons of other ways to be generous abound. Send a note of encouragement to someone. This morning I received a text from a friend of mine in New York who I haven't seen in months, just checking in and telling me how much he appreciated me. Really, he could not have done anything better to lift my spirits—it was incredibly meaningful.

We can also be generous with our listening skills, our words, our time, our talents…and the list goes on and on. Now more than ever, this generosity is needed and rare.

BEGIN LIVING SOFTLY

Let's slow down when we feel the urge to hurry. Become more mindful. Choose to breathe slowly and deeply. Be committed to relax and trust when our anxiety seems to be screaming at us. Take the time to savor life at the ultimate level. Communicate more gently with the people we love. Communicate more gently with everyone! Because we all want it and need it. Not only will theirs and our stress levels drop, we'll become more appreciative, peaceful, and patient.

BEGIN LIVING COURAGEOUSLY

Make the empowering decision to face challenges with optimism and valor and trust that "this too shall pass." When it has, we'll have the satisfaction of knowing that during that time, we consciously chose to be strong, brave, and noble. Become a pillar of strength and everyone will benefit.

Creating these habits will be difficult, especially now. But if we have the determination and persistence to start developing them now, when life has finally moved past the coronavirus and all the hysteria that accompanies it, we can gratefully look in the mirror and know that we are prepared to handle the next big challenge equally as well, or even better.

Ready to recalibrate? I'm with you, friends—we're in this together.

WAR OR PEACE

Every day, war or peace seem to be the only two choices lately. Will we fight change and the way the new normal is evolving, or will we accept life as it is now and bravely adapt to the future?

Will we anxiously jump at every bit of bad news and see it as confirmation of impending disaster and then try to resist? Or will we step back—even for a moment—and patiently, optimistically wait for life to unfold so we can respond hopefully and rationally?

This dilemma appears to be everywhere. When shopping for groceries, we may feel the conflict—thinking we must surely be infected with the coronavirus, even if we aren't. People seem to be avoiding others, making sure to keep their social distance, not looking them in the eyes…really weird, isn't it?

Our fear and insecurity seem to be magnified. When sitting alone, our mind can start playing tricks on us. Instead of using the extra time many of us now have as a gift, we may find ourselves beginning to think about random things we wish we had done differently in the past. We unnecessarily confirm to ourselves that there's so much we should have done, could have done, or ought to do next to fix things that maybe aren't even broken!

Regrets seem to abound, and fears of the future are just as prevalent. Terrifying, self-destructive thoughts seem to spring up from nowhere, for no reason—compounded by the fact that we so often feel alone during this pandemic.

Remember that if we feel as if we are stuck in inescapable quicksand or have taken a massive step backward, then that's exactly what has happened.

On the other hand, we are highly capable of making a bold choice. We can bravely choose to see that life is moving in a direction we don't understand, but we know it will eventually be better than we might imagine. Life is moving on. Life is moving forward. Always has, always will.

We can challenge our thoughts of fear, worry, dread, and guilt as they occur. We can develop thoughts and beliefs that will allow us to be beacons of peace to a world in need instead. We can look for opportunities to grow in patience, courage, determination, gratitude, and generosity, and we can crowd out the traits and thoughts that are beckoning us to join the war.

Our choice is between fearfully fighting a battle against life as it is now and the changes that are upon us, or focusing on peacefully trusting that ultimate goodness eventually lies ahead for each of us.

The decision to either fight the war or live peacefully will be offered to us every day, in many forms, so be alert. Let's choose wisely and watch the gentle ripple effects powerfully and permanently strengthen us and people around us who desperately wait for the light we can bring into their lives.

War or peace is up to each of us.

RISE UP

Perhaps there's never been a better day in our lifetime to commit to rise up. In the symbolic month of Easter, in the midst of a heartbreaking, debilitating pandemic, the world is in desperate need of our God-given abilities and gifts, and potential to rise up and overcome this immense, unprecedented challenge.

We can rise up and say loudly and clearly in a unified voice that no matter how mentally or physically battered we feel, we will ignore the pessimists and naysayers. We can continue to remain optimistic, vigilant, and resilient and inspire others to do the same.

We can rise up and give thanks for all the good we still have, while acknowledging what we and so many others have lost.

Rise up and realize that every person in every country on the globe—from Monaco to Mexico to Mozambique—has been touched somehow and likely has suffered profound pain. Let's empathize with that pain, more genuinely and ardently than ever.

Let's take our differences off the table and instead rise up and be grateful for the foundation of freedom we all have to choose our own way and to seek happiness and fulfillment, regardless of our race, religion, or political beliefs.

Let's proactively put our real or perceived needs aside, rise up, and reach out to our friends, family, and others who want and need to hear from us.

Let's rise up and authentically pray for peace and healing and kindness, knowing that words of prayer are the most powerful healers in the world.

We can rise up and bravely choose to overcome our personal regrets and self-judgement for what may have happened in the past. Let's gently remind ourselves that we did the best we could at the time and use that understanding to offer our gifts in a renewed way to others that are likely fighting battles we can scarcely imagine.

Let's rise up and find creative ways to use this experience to our benefit—to make or remake ourselves into the stronger, wiser, more compassionate people that we long to be.

Regardless of where we are in the world, let's join together and boldly rise up in faith and love and courage. A better or more crucial time in history to do so may never arise.

MORE STRENGTH, LESS STRESS

Times have certainly changed. Better stay six feet away. Better make a run to stock up. Better learn how to do everything online. Better hoard toilet paper. It's as if we are being programmed to think that we are really out of luck everywhere we look.

EVERYTHING SEEMS TO BE ONE BIG, STRESSFUL PROBLEM.

Today, let's change that. Life in the new normal is going to be different for sure, but there is still time to come out of this whole thing with powerful personal growth and strength under our belts. In fact, I'll bet you have secretly wanted to improve in some of the following areas for a long, long time. Now is a golden opportunity, so let's get busy!

LEARN TO LOWER THE BAR FOR LETTING GO

It's time to start realizing that we really don't have a lot of control over life, and that's okay.

Now is the time to make peace with that uncertainty. We can learn to be comfortable with not knowing and use this time to teach ourselves to steer the boat—but accept that we can't steer the river.

We have been walking around in a chronic state of worry, tension, and stress for who knows how long trying to control every aspect of life, so let's give ourselves permission to let go and embrace the fact that we might not know exactly what the future will look like. Regardless of how it goes, we will adapt and grow stronger through it if we choose to do so.

BECOME A BONA FIDE AMAZING LISTENER

Hear me out: Now is the time to practice and perfect this one skill that will set you apart from the majority of people. You'll become more appreciated, less self-conscious, and more knowledgeable by listening more than you speak. Research shows that good listeners are perceived as more attractive than people who constantly talk about themselves!

Good listening is a manifestation of self-confidence, security, and trust. If you take the time and make the effort to genuinely hear someone out, you demonstrate that you trust that your situation and challenges will be handled. This frees you up to focus on hearing the *other* person's needs.

In fact, nothing makes another person feel as valued as when someone gives them their undivided attention and assures them that they know exactly what they mean. Now is the time to become like that—trust me, you won't regret it.

BECOME A PROBLEM SOLVER

Now is a great time to start believing you are bigger than anything that life will throw at you. Don't just give up or sell yourself short when you stumble across a situation that would typically defeat you. Push yourself a little. Then a little more. See this situation as a challenge to be solved instead of a problem to be delegated because you don't immediately know how to respond to it.

Let's show ourselves and others how resourceful we are. Even Einstein said, "It's not that I'm so smart, it's that I stay with problems longer."

If someone told you in the past that you weren't capable, now is the time to break free from those chains. Don't let their criticism or vocal doubt in your abilities hold you back anymore or stop you from trying. Follow the directions. Or heck, create your own directions. Google it. Didn't work on the first try? Oh well, try again. And again. And again. Eventually you'll get it right. Nowadays more than ever, we can figure out things or fix things we never dreamed we could, and our confidence will rise each time we do. Got a problem? You can solve it.

***

These three skills can make you feel happier, more confident, and more empowered as you develop them. I can't think of a better time than now to start, so let's get going!

PROCEED TO THE (NEW) ROUTE

The Atlanta traffic was…horrible and made even worse because my GPS had sent me down a road that I seldom used while traveling in the city.

As soon as I realized I had missed the next turn onto another side street, I heard those dreaded words: "Proceed to the route." Then again, "Proceed to the route."

In the midst of navigating unfamiliar side streets and not knowing how to get back to where my gadget suggested I go, I laughed and blurted out to my trusty GPS assistant, "Look, this is the NEW route, okay?" I continued until I found the exact street that would get me back to where I needed to be, and the GPS stopped its constant, annoying chatter.

Suddenly I realized the similarities between that situation and the one we all face. We are all proceeding to a "new route." We are all headed toward uncharted territory on roads we aren't familiar with. But even when the route sometimes gets frustrating and scary, we'll figure it out. We'll get back on track. Because life will go on and we will go on too.

In fact, our new route may turn out to be better than the old one. We may discover beautiful scenery we wouldn't have seen otherwise. We will likely meet new, inspiring people that we might never have met. We will probably learn things about ourselves on this route that we would never have learned any other way.

One thing is for sure: We decide how we respond to the new route. We decide how much courage we will show on our new journey. We decide where we will go as we approach this new frontier. We can choose to blaze a new and potentially better trail compassionately, faithfully, and powerfully. No one else will do it for us. In fact, we wouldn't want anyone else to do it for us.

Yes, the journey we will go on will be ours alone to navigate, and we are ready. Sure, we hope to receive help and support along the way from friends and family, but ultimately, *we* get to recalibrate this new normal and start over. Clear the slate.

Hopefully, we have learned new lessons about simplicity, kindness, determination, and patience during this pandemic. Because if we have, they will provide us with fuel and direction that will make our journey more authentic and make the ultimate destination clearer.

The end of the quarantine is approaching for most of us. Let's emerge mentally, physically, and spiritually prepared to seize this new time with optimism and faith, trusting the adventure ahead of us will be fulfilling, unique, and empowering.

Proceed to the route, friends. Good roads are ahead.

***

CAN I ASK A FAVOR?

First of all, thank you for reading my book! Would you do me a favor and take a moment to write a short review on Amazon? Reviews are so important to authors like me and if you would share your thoughts so others can find out about my writing, I would be truly grateful. If you do, feel free to let me know by dropping me an email at skipjohnsonauthor1@gmail.com so I can tell you thanks!

ABOUT THE AUTHOR

Skip Johnson is an inspirational author and speaker whose goal is to inspire and empower his audiences to live happier, more successful lives. As a business leader, Skip practices what he preaches about attitude and happiness. As part of his family's health club chain in Georgia for thirty-five years, Skip helped steer the clubs to earning numerous national and international awards, including Best Customer Service Club Worldwide out of more than 700 locations by Gold's Gym International in 2000. In addition to *Hidden Jewels of Happiness*, he is the author of inspirational books *Grateful for Everything* and *Starting Each Day in a Powerful Way*. Skip is an accomplished storyteller and best known for his motivational and educational talks that focus on exploring leaders' potential to influence culture and increase happiness. He has also earned the designation of Master Tennis Professional, one held by less than one percent of 16,000 USPTA certified tennis professionals internationally. Skip lives outside of Atlanta, Georgia with his wife, Anne Marie. To read his other books, ebooks, and articles, to learn more about him and his newest writings, or to book speaking engagements, visit skipjohnsonauthor.com. For daily inspiration, visit facebook.com/SkipJohnsonAuthor.